Fruit for Christ's Labour

Yannick Ford

Scripture Truth Publications

FRUIT FOR CHRIST'S LABOUR

FIRST EDITION

FIRST PRINTING July 2015

ISBN: 978-0-901860-74-3 (paperback)

Copyright © 2015 Yannick Ford and Scripture Truth Publications

A publication of Scripture Truth

All rights reserved. No part of this publication may be reproduced, stored in a retrieval system, or transmitted, in any form or by any means, electronic, mechanical, photocopying, recording or otherwise without prior permission of Scripture Truth Publications.

Unless otherwise indicated, Scriptures are taken from the New King James Version®. Copyright © 1979, 1980, 1982 by Thomas Nelson, Inc. Used by permission. All rights reserved.
(The British usage text was first published as the Revised Authorised Version by Samuel Bagster and Sons Ltd., London, in 1982).

The Scripture quotation referred to as being from the English Standard Version is from The ESV® Bible (The Holy Bible, English Standard Version®), copyright © 2001 by Crossway, a publishing ministry of Good News Publishers. Used by permission. All rights reserved.

Quotation from *We Would See Jesus* by Roy Hession by permission of the Roy Hession Book Trust © Roy Hession Book Trust 1950, United Kingdom.

Published by Scripture Truth Publications
31-33 Glover Street, Crewe, Cheshire, CW1 3LD

Scripture Truth is an imprint of Central Bible Hammond Trust, a charitable trust

Typesetting by John Rice
Printed by Lightning Source

FRUIT FOR CHRIST'S LABOUR

*Affectionately dedicated to my parents,
John and Fabienne Ford*

FRUIT FOR CHRIST'S LABOUR

CONTENTS

Acknowledgements 6
Foreword 7
Introduction 9
Chapter 1   Our Problem 13
Chapter 2   The Fulfilment of the Scriptures 23
Chapter 3   Our Father 33
Chapter 4   The Glorious Man 43
Chapter 5   The Great High Priest 49
Chapter 6   The Man of Joy 59
Conclusion Putting it All Together 68
Appendix   Who is Jesus? 71
Notes 79

Acknowledgements

*For all things come from You, and of Your own
we have given You (1 Chronicles 29:14).*

Many people have helped me produce this book, and I am grateful to them all. I thank Joanne Sher for her most helpful and comprehensive editing of my manuscripts. Theo Balderston carefully reviewed the initial draft and gave me many valuable suggestions. David Taylor made time in his busy schedule for helpful comments, as did John Broadley and John Rice. John Rice also did all the hard work of getting the manuscript ready for publication! I wish to thank my wife Rachel for all her encouragement, support and enthusiastic reviews of the various drafts.

This book is about the Lord Jesus Christ, and I hope that I have spoken of Him "what is right", in the spirit of Job 42:7. May He be glorified in all things!

Foreword

Who then is a faithful and wise servant, whom his master made ruler over his household, to give them food in due season? Blessed is that servant whom his master, when he comes, will find so doing (Matthew 24:45-46).

However, Jesus did not permit him, but said to him, "Go home to your friends, and tell them what great things the Lord has done for you, and how He has had compassion on you" (Mark 5:19).

These Scriptures declare the importance of spiritual food to God's people, and the need to speak well of God and His grace to those who do not yet know Him personally. I have often felt the force of these words, and this book is an attempt to discharge some of that responsibility.

The Lord Jesus said of Himself, "I am the bread of life. He who comes to Me shall never hunger, and he who believes in Me shall never thirst" (John 6:35). Therefore, to write about Him is in one sense to provide food for His people. Furthermore, His words are words of welcome. They are an invitation to come and see, and to taste that the Lord is good. My desire is that you will experience something of the greatness of His work and of His love as you consider the fruits of His labour. Of course what I have written falls far short of His glory, but I trust that it will encourage you to explore the marvellous ways of God's grace.

Introduction

He shall see the labour of His soul, and be satisfied. By His knowledge My righteous Servant shall justify many, for He shall bear their iniquities (Isaiah 53:11).

When I was learning biology at school, my teacher used to say that a good picture was worth a thousand words. Consequently he encouraged the class to draw biological diagrams when answering questions. It is true that a good picture is often better than a lengthy piece of text – so long as the picture does its job properly. I am sure that many of my readers have been frustrated with instruction leaflets where the photograph or diagram of the object to be built was anything but clear and helpful!

If you buy a Bible today, it may well include illustrations, drawings and maps. These, of course, are not part of the inspired text, but they can be quite helpful. Nevertheless, the inspired text does have pictures of a different sort. They are what I call "word pictures", and they help us to understand some of the great themes of the Bible.

These great themes are brought to us in several different ways. There is formal, step-by-step teaching, such as in the letters of the apostle Paul. Then there are the word pictures which include the parables that Jesus told, the historical records, and the allegories and visions recorded in the Old Testament. By putting all of these together, we get a much richer understanding of what God wants us to know. Crucially, we learn to know God Himself better.

To know God better is a compelling reason to study Bible themes from many different angles. I want to look at some word pictures that illustrate the great consequences of Christ's death and resurrection. In so doing we will see something of His wonderful character as we consider what He delights in. The purpose of our study will be to have a renewed and strengthened affection for our Lord Jesus as we think about the fruit of His work.

It goes without saying that Christ's death and resurrection are of prime importance. In 1 Corinthians 15:3-4, the apostle Paul writes, "For I delivered to you first of all that which I also received: that Christ died for our sins according to the Scriptures, and that He was buried, and that He rose again the third day according to the Scriptures." The English Standard Version translates verse 3 as "For I delivered unto you **as of first importance** ..." (emphasis mine). Christians know and believe that Christ suffered the penalty for their sins when He died on the cross. They know that Christ's resurrection proves that His death for them has been accepted – their Substitute has met the demands of justice against them in full. This is wonderful news, and like a well-cut gemstone that can be admired from many different angles, the results of Christ's death on

INTRODUCTION

the cross are displayed in several different word pictures all through the Bible. Isaiah 53 is one example. Indeed it was through reading this very chapter that an Ethiopian official was converted. Acts 8 tells us about his conversion. We read there that the Ethiopian official asked Philip the evangelist to explain to him what the prophet Isaiah was writing about:

> "I ask you, of whom does the prophet say this, of himself or of some other man?" Then Philip opened his mouth, and beginning at this Scripture, preached Jesus to him.
>
> **Acts 8:34-35**

The answer to his question, "Of whom does the prophet say this?" was "Jesus." Philip explained that the servant spoken of in Isaiah 53 was in fact a picture of the Lord Jesus. Further down in the same chapter, we read that Jesus will see "the fruit of the travail of His soul" (Isaiah 53:11) – the fruit of His labour, as we might say today.

It is wonderful to think of the Lord Jesus enjoying the fruit of His work! What is astonishing is that much of this fruit in which He rejoices also involves our blessing. He rejoices in the results of His work, and these results are the foundation for our eternal happiness!

Let us therefore explore some of that fruit of the Lord Jesus' work. Some of the chapters are based on a New Testament text, and some from the Old Testament. The New Testament gives us the teaching that we need to understand the scope and results of Christ's work. The Old Testament gives us some precious insights into motives and emotions of our Lord that might otherwise have been hidden.

The great themes of the calling of the church, the Bride of Christ, and the restoration of God's own people Israel are not addressed here. This is not because they are not important – on the contrary, they are truly a special part of the fruit of Jesus' work. The focus of this book has been restricted to consider some of the ways in which the Lord Jesus relates to us individually, with the aim of encouraging a greater appreciation of His love to us.

Whilst this book is intended to be an encouragement to Christians, I trust that it may also be helpful to those who do not yet know the Lord Jesus in a personal way, but are curious to find out more. If that describes you, you may wish to jump straight to the appendix at the end of this book. There you may see for yourself what Christ has done for you. The rest of the book will then make more sense.

Chapter 1
Our Problem

If You, LORD, should mark iniquities, O Lord, who could stand? But there is forgiveness with You, that You may be feared (Psalm 130:3-4).

Thankfully, I have never yet had to appear in a court of law. If I received a summons, I would certainly need a clear head and strong nerves, whether I was giving a witness statement, acting as a member of the jury, or defending myself against a charge.

We see something of this kind of drama in the Old Testament book of the prophet Zechariah, chapter 3, although the event described is not necessarily a court scene.

> Then he showed me Joshua the high priest standing before the Angel of the LORD, and Satan standing at his right hand to oppose him. And the LORD said to Satan, "The LORD rebuke you, Satan! The LORD who has chosen Jerusalem rebuke you! Is this not a brand plucked from the fire?" Now Joshua was clothed with filthy garments, and was standing before the Angel. Then He answered and spoke to those who stood before Him, saying, "Take

away the filthy garments from him." And to him He said, "See, I have removed your iniquity from you, and I will clothe you with rich robes." And I said, "Let them put a clean turban on his head." So they put a clean turban on his head, and they put the clothes on him. And the Angel of the LORD stood by.

Zechariah 3:1-5

Let us briefly review the context of Zechariah's prophecy. Zechariah was alive in the period after the Jewish exile in Babylon. He had returned to the land of Israel with the former exiles, and the temple was being re-built in Jerusalem. The people needed much encouragement, because they were surrounded by hostile nations that did not want Jerusalem to be restored.

The first six chapters of Zechariah describe a number of visions that were given to him, showing how God was going to bless Jerusalem once again. The city and temple would be re-built, and Jerusalem's enemies would be confounded. Chapter six ends with a wonderful prediction of the Messiah who will sit as a priest upon His throne. In this way, God outlined His plans for His people. These visions must have been a great encouragement to the small group of exiles who had returned home.

The vision of Joshua the high priest comes in the middle of the series. There we see Joshua acting as a representative of his people. We notice a great and serious problem – Joshua appears in most unsuitable clothing. He is clothed in filthy garments! How can he possibly come before God like that?

It is amazing what difference clothes can make. How awkward we can feel if we think that we are over-dressed or under-dressed! I once had to deliver some raw material to a processing plant for a trial. I thought that the company would have no problem making my sample, so I happily went off for lunch, expecting to turn up later and simply pick up my sample. Instead, I walked into a rather bad atmosphere. The material had caused problems and the workers were annoyed! I was wearing a smart shirt, jacket and tie, which all got covered in sticky rosemary powder as I tried to help out with the issue. It was not the best way to dress for the circumstances!

At the other end of the scale, I remember feeling underdressed at a trade show, where everyone else seemed to be wearing sharp suits. I was rather conscious of my shoes, which had sustained some damage because I had dropped some caustic solution on them in the laboratory, and which I had not-too-successfully tried to cover up with polish!

My errors in choosing suitable clothes are amusing memories for me now, but the filthy clothes that Joshua was wearing pointed to a far more serious situation. They were a picture of sin, as we can see from verse 4 of Zechariah 3:

> Then He answered and spoke to those who stood before Him, saying, "Take away the filthy garments from him." And to him He said, "See, I have removed your iniquity from you, and I will clothe you with rich robes."

What we have in Zechariah's vision is a beautiful word picture showing how God removes our sin from us. In order to appreciate this picture better, we must take a more detailed look at the vision and the main players in it.

The vision starts abruptly, with three characters introduced: the Angel of the LORD, Joshua the high priest, and Satan. The expression 'Angel of the LORD' needs some explanation. This name appears quite often in the Old Testament, and is used for a manifestation of God Himself. A good example is found in Exodus 3:2, which describes the time when Moses came to the burning bush:

> And the Angel of the LORD appeared to him in a flame of fire from the midst of a bush. So he looked, and behold, the bush was burning with fire, but the bush was not consumed.

Moses was intrigued by this strange sight and went to look more closely. Exodus 3:4-6 shows us that the Angel of the LORD was indeed God, since the voice from the bush said, "I am the God of your father – the God of Abraham, the God of Isaac, and the God of Jacob." Other instances of this name in the Old Testament show us the same thing: for example, the Angel of the LORD whose name was 'Wonderful' (compare Judges 13:17-19 with Isaiah 9:6).

As well as the Angel of the LORD, Satan is also mentioned. Furthermore, we read that Satan was there to oppose Joshua. The word 'Satan' actually means an opponent or an adversary. His name and the verb 'to oppose' are from the same source.[1] In English, you could say "the opponent standing at his right hand to oppose him."

What a terrible situation! Imagine being in God's presence, but having such a powerful and terrible adversary there at the same time, trying to make sure that you will forfeit all blessing, and be condemned by God instead! It would be like being in court and having a powerful and clever prosecuting attorney determined to see you condemned.

OUR PROBLEM

In what way was Satan opposing Joshua? The text doesn't say so explicitly, but we can see what it was from the context as we read on. We have already seen that Joshua was wearing filthy garments, and that the removal of the filthy garments was a picture of sin being removed. Joshua, as the high priest, symbolised the nation of Israel standing before God in their sin. And *we* are like that too! If left to ourselves, we too would only have filthy garments in which to appear before God.

This situation gives Satan the ammunition he needs. He is the one who accuses, which is why he is shown in the vision as the one standing to oppose Joshua. If we read Revelation 12 9-10, we will see that he is named plainly there as *the accuser of our brethren*:

> So the great dragon was cast out, that serpent of old, called the Devil and Satan, who deceives the whole world; he was cast to the earth, and his angels were cast out with him. Then I heard a loud voice saying in heaven, "Now salvation, and strength, and the kingdom of our God, and the power of His Christ have come, for the accuser of our brethren, who accused them before our God day and night, has been cast down."

When Satan accuses us, he is of course aiming at us, but he is principally *aiming at God*. It is as if he is saying, "How can You be a holy and just God, if You bless these sinful people? How does that square with Your justice? But if You condemn them, where is Your love?"

It is a fearful situation. If we had been there, in Joshua's place, we would have felt that we had nowhere to hide, and no excuse to give. How could we possibly deliver ourselves from such a powerful accuser? Our own filthy garments would have testified against us!

Satan does not need to invent false accusations, because there are plenty of things in our own lives that he can bring up against us, to show that we are utterly unworthy of any blessing. Pause a moment and think about these things. God is real. His holiness and hatred of sin are real. Our opponent is real, and our sins are real. Zechariah's vision is not just an interesting story. It pictures important truths that concern us.

Thankfully, the vision does not stop there. As we read on, we can see how God deals with this problem. I want to think about four things in particular:

- What Joshua says and does,
- What the Angel of the LORD says and does,
- The reasons that the Angel of the LORD gives, and
- How Satan responds.

Firstly, what does Joshua say and do? The simple answer is nothing! He does not say anything, and he does not do anything. He does not try to give an excuse for his filthy clothes, nor does he try to rebut Satan's accusation. This is very striking. He has no excuse, but he relies absolutely on God.

It is the same with us. We *are* sinners – the Word of God declares it. Therefore if Satan accuses us of sin, we already know it is true – but we also know that God can forgive. "If You, LORD, should mark iniquities, O Lord, who could stand? But there is forgiveness with You, That You may be feared" (Psalm 130:3-4). "For if our heart condemns us, God is greater than our heart, and knows all things" (1 John 3:20).

But, secondly, whereas Joshua is silent, the Angel of the LORD speaks. He rebukes Satan, and then He insists on His right to choose Jerusalem, and His right to pluck a brand out of the fire. He removes the filthy clothes from

Joshua, and clothes him with rich robes, signifying the removal of Joshua's iniquity, and his being credited with God's righteousness. What a beautiful picture of our salvation this is! The Lord has done everything for us! Consider the words of the apostle Paul to Titus:

> But when the kindness and the love of God our Saviour toward man appeared, not by works of righteousness which we have done, but according to His mercy He saved us, through the washing of regeneration and renewing of the Holy Spirit, whom He poured out on us abundantly through Jesus Christ our Saviour, that having been justified by His grace we should become heirs according to the hope of eternal life.
>
> **Titus 3:4-7**

Thirdly, we see the reason that the Angel of the LORD gives for His actions. It is simply this – He insists on His right to choose! What peace and assurance this gives! If God has chosen us, it is because of His own love and grace. It has nothing to do with our own worthiness. We might be the "chief of sinners" as the apostle Paul calls himself, yet the grace of God reaches us!

The Bible tells us that "the heart is deceitful above all things, and desperately wicked" (Jeremiah 17:9). We do not always realise the full extent of this when we are converted, and we may have to learn this painful truth as we go on in our Christian lives. As we begin to understand just how wicked the human heart is, we can be so thankful that God chose us in spite of what we were, purely according to His love and grace.

Fourthly, we see that Satan does not say anything in reply. This is also truly encouraging. God has spoken, and He has insisted on His choice. This reminds us of the protection from condemnation that the apostle Paul wrote about to the Romans:

> Who shall bring a charge against God's elect? It is God who justifies. Who is he who condemns? It is Christ who died, and furthermore is also risen, who is even at the right hand of God, who also makes intercession for us.
>
> **Romans 8:33-34**

Once Joshua has been clothed in rich robes and has had the clean turban placed on his head, he is admonished to walk in God's ways. Let us read on in Zechariah chapter 3:

> Then the Angel of the LORD admonished Joshua, saying, "Thus says the LORD of hosts: 'If you will walk in My ways, and if you will keep My command, then you shall also judge My house, and likewise have charge of My courts; I will give you places to walk among these who stand here.'"
>
> **Zechariah 3:6-7**

We can see a beautiful parallel with our salvation. First of all, we need to have our sins dealt with. We need to have righteousness credited to us, a righteousness that we neither earned nor deserved, but that we desperately need. Only then can we start to walk in God's ways. We have the same order of events in Ephesians 2:8-10:

> For by grace you have been saved through faith, and that not of yourselves; it is the gift of God, not of works, lest anyone should boast. For we are His workmanship, created in Christ Jesus for good works, which God prepared beforehand that we should walk in them.

So what do we gain from a study of Zechariah's vision? How does it help us to better understand and appreciate our salvation? It brings several truths home to us in a dramatic way:

- The seriousness of our situation
- The reality of our enemy and his accusations
- The supremely comforting fact that God chooses us and forgives us according to His sovereign grace, and not according to our merit.

It also helps us to understand the righteousness that we are given when we trust in Christ. Joshua was *given* clean, rich robes. We may not always *feel* righteous, but we can remember that it is a gift of God, and does not depend on us or our feelings.

Now of course Zechariah 3 does not explain *how* God can forgive righteously, nor *how* He can remove iniquity and clothe with righteousness without injustice to His holiness. We have to turn to other passages in the Bible to see this, but as we know from the New Testament, God's holiness and hatred of sin have been fully satisfied in the death of our Lord Jesus on the cross. Even in the Old Testament we have clear pictures of this; for example, in the well-loved 53rd chapter of Isaiah.

> But He was wounded for our transgressions, He was bruised for our iniquities; the chastisement for our peace was upon Him, and by His stripes we are healed. All we like sheep have gone astray; we have turned, every one, to his own way; and the LORD has laid on Him the iniquity of us all.
>
> **Isaiah 53:5-6**

Zechariah's vision helps us appreciate this salvation, by seeing in a dramatic word picture how sin is dealt with in the courts of heaven. It is remarkable to think that this is one aspect of the fruit of Jesus' labour. Jesus came "to seek and to save that which was lost". His death on the cross and His resurrection mean that He can freely bless those who trust in Him. He is free to save! Zechariah's vision helps us to understand how comprehensive, secure and certain our salvation is.

QUESTIONS FOR REFLECTION

- Joshua the high priest was a real person, and obviously would have been aware of Zechariah's vision. How do you think he felt about it? How would you have felt about it if it had been you who had been seen in that vision?
- In what way does Zechariah's vision help you to better appreciate what God has done for you through the work of the Lord Jesus?
- How do you see yourself – as someone standing before God in filthy clothes, or as someone clothed in Christ's righteousness which He has given to you?

Chapter 2
The Fulfilment
of the Scriptures

*These are the words which I spoke to you
while I was still with you, that all things must be
fulfilled which were written in the Law of Moses
and the Prophets and the Psalms concerning Me
(Luke 24:44).*

I am very fond of poetry. I was not always fond of it – as a schoolboy I sometimes found poetry very tiresome! I still remember having to write comments in an end-of-year exam on some impenetrable poem. It seemed to me then that a poem could only be considered "good" if it was more or less impossible to understand.

What I have come to realise is that truly good poetry is not difficult to comprehend. Instead, it expresses important concepts in few words, with those few words allowing you to *feel* it. One of my favourite poetry collections is a small, two volume work called *Hymns of Ter Steegen, Suso and Others*, translated and compiled by Emma Frances Bevan in the nineteenth century. One poem struck me greatly, and I quote part of it here:[2]

Thou knowest the sun by his glory—
Thou knowest the rose by her breath,
Thou knowest the fire by its glowing—
Thou knowest My love by death.

Wouldst thou know in My great creation
Where the rays of My glory meet?
Where to My awful righteousness
The kiss of My peace is sweet?
Where shine forth the wisdom and wonder
Of God's everlasting plan?
Behold on the cross of dishonour
A cursed and a dying Man.

It was the last two lines quoted above that made me stop and wonder. They formed such a contrast to what came before. We read about the sun, the rose, the fire, creation, glory, righteousness, peace, wisdom and wonder – and then those terrible words, "Behold on the cross of dishonour / A cursed and a dying Man." Admittedly the phrase "Thou knowest My love by death" came earlier, but still, the thoughts of the "cross of dishonour" and "a cursed and a dying Man" came as a shock.

Similar things came as a shock to the two disciples who were walking to Emmaus, as we read in Luke 24:13-35. Jesus Himself joined these two and spoke with them, but at first they did not know that it was He. He listened to them and drew out their sorrows. "We were hoping", they said, "that it was He [i.e. Jesus] who was going to redeem Israel." Instead, as they had already sadly said, "the chief priests and our rulers delivered Him to be condemned to death, and crucified Him."

What did Jesus say in response? He did not at first reveal who He was, but He pointed the disciples to the Scriptures: "Then He said to them, 'O foolish ones, and slow of heart to believe in all that the prophets have spoken! Ought not the Christ to have suffered these things and to enter into His glory?' And beginning at Moses and all the Prophets, He expounded to them in all the Scriptures the things concerning Himself" (Luke 24:25-27).

Later on that day, when the Lord had shown Himself to all the disciples, He said again, "These are the words which I spoke to you while I was still with you, that all things must be fulfilled which were written in the Law of Moses and the Prophets and the Psalms concerning Me" (Luke 24:44).

This brings us to another aspect of the fruit of the Lord Jesus' work – the fulfilment of the Scriptures. For the Lord Jesus, the Scriptures were of prime importance. He Himself had said, "The Scripture cannot be broken" (John 10:35). All things written about Him had to be accomplished. Indeed, it is striking how often we meet expressions such as "the Scripture was fulfilled", "it is written", or "have you not read" when we read the Gospels. The Lord's earthly life was truly governed by the Scriptures.

And yet, what Scriptures these were that had to come to pass! Certainly there were Scriptures of the glory that He would enter into, but also Scriptures concerning His sufferings. For example, consider the following texts[3]:

> ... that it might be fulfilled which was spoken by Isaiah the prophet, saying:
>
> > *"He Himself took our infirmities*
> > *And bore our sicknesses."*
> >
> > **Matthew 8:17**
>
> Then they crucified Him, and divided His garments, casting lots, that it might be fulfilled which was spoken by the prophet:

FRUIT FOR CHRIST'S LABOUR

> *"They divided My garments among them,*
> *And for My clothing they cast lots."*
> **Matthew 27:35**

What terrible Scriptures these were that He needed to complete! What sufferings lay ahead of our Saviour when He was here on earth, waiting for His work on the cross. No wonder He once said, "But I have a baptism to be baptized with, and how distressed I am till it is accomplished!" (Luke 12:50). But the Lord Jesus had also said, "Ought not the Christ to have suffered these things and to enter into His glory?"

After the Saviour had passed triumphantly through death and judgement, what wonderful Scriptures could now be fulfilled in Him! As He had accomplished the Scriptures concerning His sufferings to the letter, so now the Scriptures concerning the glorious fruit of His labour could come to pass. For instance, consider the following examples:

- Our sins are forgiven, *according to the Scriptures* (1 Corinthians 15:3-4).
- God is able to impute righteousness and justify the ungodly, *according to the Scriptures* (Romans 4:3-6).
- All who trust in Jesus can be guaranteed to be saved, *according to the Scriptures* (Romans 10:11).
- The Gentiles can come into blessing, *according to the Scriptures* (Galatians 3:8-9).
- God's ancient people, Israel, will also come into blessing, and all Israel will be saved, *according to the Scriptures* (Romans 11:25-27).

As we pause and consider these Scriptures – the ones that testified of the suffering that awaited the Saviour, and the ones that testified of the glorious results that would follow – we marvel at the greatness of the work

THE FULFILMENT OF THE SCRIPTURES

of our Lord Jesus, and the greatness of His Person. What a Saviour we have, who was willing to accomplish all these Scriptures, so that we could come into the blessing of the results of His work.

We should pause to consider how was it that Jesus was able to fulfil the Scriptures concerning His sufferings. How did He have the strength of purpose never to turn aside from His work? We have some clues from the Scriptures themselves. In Hebrews 12:2, we read that He, "for the joy that was set before Him endured the cross, despising the shame, and has sat down at the right hand of the throne of God."

He knew of the joy that was set before Him – the joy of glorifying His Father who had been so dishonoured because of sin, the joy of redeeming a people who would now worship the Father in spirit and in truth, the joy of accomplishing our redemption and setting us free, and the joy of procuring a people for Himself who would become His bride. All of these things were testified to in the Scriptures. Hebrews 10:5-7, a passage that explains the prophecy of Psalm 40, provides an interesting insight:

> Therefore, when He came into the world, He said:
> *"Sacrifice and offering You did not desire,*
> *But a body You have prepared for Me.*
> *In burnt offerings and sacrifices for sin*
> *You had no pleasure.*
> *Then I said, 'Behold, I have come—*
> *In the volume of the book it is written of Me—*
> *To do Your will, O God.'"*
> **Hebrews 10:5-7**

"In the volume of the Book" – in the Scriptures – it was written of Him. I am sure that it was His unswerving faith in the Scriptures that sustained Him in those dark hours on the cross when He was suffering for our sins. We have no real understanding of what happened in those three dark hours, when God turned His face away. Until then, the Lord Jesus, as a Man on earth, had always been in communion with His God and Father. But on the cross, when He was made sin for us, we hear His cry, again quoted from the Scriptures, "My God, My God, why have You forsaken Me?" (Matthew 27:46; Psalm 22:1).

We have never been forsaken by God. Perhaps it has felt like that on occasion, but it has never really been so. Jeremiah must have felt like that at times, as we see from his Lamentations: "I am the man who has seen affliction by the rod of His wrath. He has led me and made me walk in darkness and not in light" (Lamentations 3:1-2). However, only Jesus could have said in all its fullness that *He* was the Man who saw affliction by the rod of God's wrath.

What could have sustained our Saviour as He entered into that awful darkness? Imagine for a moment entering into a time when you really were forsaken by God. He would not regard you nor hear your prayer, and you would feel the full weight of your sins, and the awful truth that God's anger against your sins was fully deserved. In the language of Jeremiah's Lamentations 3:1-8, God was turning His hand against you, hedging you in so that you could not get out, and your prayer was shut out. What confidence would you have of ever getting out of that situation? Conscience would accuse, your prayers would not be heard, and the terrors of the evil one would add to your sorrow. In a sense in which we cannot enter into, our Saviour suffered this.

The answer must lie in the Scriptures, those Scriptures that He trusted in and fulfilled to the letter. Psalm 16 provides a clue. It is quoted in Acts 2:25-28, where Peter explains clearly that this psalm is about Jesus.

> Therefore my heart is glad, and my glory rejoices;
> My flesh also will rest in hope.
> For You will not leave my soul in Sheol,
> Nor will You allow Your Holy One to see corruption.
> You will show me the path of life;
> In Your presence is fullness of joy;
> At Your right hand are pleasures for evermore.
>
> **Psalm 16:9-11**

"You will show me the path of life." Even in the midst of the darkness, when in grace He was made sin for us and suffered the righteous penalty of our sins, this Scripture remained true – the Scripture that "cannot be broken" (John 10:35). There was nothing to sustain Him then but the Scriptures, but these were wonderfully proved. Our Lord won the victory. He passed through triumphantly. He accomplished all the Scriptures that foretold His suffering, so that the Scriptures that foretold His glory and our blessing could be fulfilled. These Scriptures that speak of His glory are very much part of the fruit of His labour. Through grace, we come into rich blessing thereby. Shall we not praise and adore Him?

A Practical Application — Our Response

If the fulfilment of the Scriptures, including those that concern our blessing, are part of the fruit of the Lord Jesus' work, how should we respond? In the words of Psalm 116:12, "What shall I render to the Lord for all His benefits toward me?" Here are three possible responses:

Firstly, we must trust only in His work – not in our own righteousness. The apostle Paul wrote in his letter to the Philippians that he wanted to "be found in Him, not having my own righteousness, which is from the law, but that which is through faith in Christ, the righteousness which is from God by faith" (Philippians 3:9). Our righteousness has been procured for us at great cost. There was no way that we could have worked our own righteousness, and now we must not seek to be accepted on our own merits. It is the Saviour who makes us righteous. Therefore Paul said earlier in the same letter, "we are the circumcision, who worship God in the Spirit, rejoice in Christ Jesus, and have no confidence in the flesh" (Philippians 3:3).

To rejoice in Christ Jesus means boasting in Him, thankful that *He* has been successful where we have failed, and trusting entirely in His work. We have no confidence in our own flesh – that sinful flesh which made it necessary for Jesus to die on the cross – but we rejoice in Him! He will be our strength.

> But of Him you are in Christ Jesus, who became for us wisdom from God—and righteousness and sanctification and redemption—that, as it is written, "*He who glories, let him glory in the* LORD."
>
> 1 Corinthians 1:30-31

Secondly, we should not make light of sin. Proverbs 14:9 tells us, "Fools mock at sin, but among the upright there is favour." When we consider what the Lord Jesus went through because of our sin, we realise that there simply is no room to make light of sin. It is not funny, nor a laughing matter. Sin brought our Lord to the cross and to the three hours of darkness. It was not funny then, and it is not funny now.

We must remember however that we are not sinless now – "If we say that we have no sin, we deceive ourselves, and the truth is not in us" (1 John 1:8). Nevertheless, when we sin, we know that we are forgiven and that we can be brought back into practical fellowship with our Father: "If we confess our sins, He is faithful and just to forgive us our sins and to cleanse us from all unrighteousness" (1 John 1:9). There is full provision for us – forgiveness, cleansing and restoration. But let us remember that sin is not a laughing matter. "Fools mock at sin."

Thirdly, our testimony about the Lord should be, "I have found." In *We Would See Jesus*, Roy Hession expresses it as follows:

> He has found at last where the true gold is, and has sunk his shaft into that precious vein, the Lord Jesus. He is not now shaken or disturbed by the report of "lucky strikes" anywhere else – in this doctrine or that experience, or in some other emphasis.[4]

Here we have a metaphor of gold mining. In this illustration, the gold miner had found a rich seam, and consequently was not interested in other reports of "lucky strikes", since he had already found the real thing. What Hession expresses so well has the ring of truth about it. We have found peace, joy, forgiveness, love and blessing in our Lord Jesus. What He has done has procured all this and more for us. He has fulfilled the Scriptures and we rest on His work. All the glory must go to Him!

QUESTIONS FOR REFLECTION

- Why was it important that Christ fulfilled the Scriptures?

- How does that encourage us now?
- What confidence does it give us in those Scriptures that are yet to be fulfilled?

Chapter 3
Our Father

I am ascending to My Father and your Father, and to My God and your God (John 20:17).

I love to browse in second-hand bookshops. Sometimes there is nothing of interest on the shelves, but if the shop is well-stocked I may well find something that takes my fancy. Usually the price is low enough for me to take a risk on a book! It was in a second-hand bookshop in Switzerland that I found a collection of Adolphe Monod's sermons. Monod was a preacher in France in the 19th century, and one of his quotes particularly appeals to me as a writer: "Lord, direct my pen, and give me thoughts and words that can glorify Your Name, feed Your people and convert sinners."[5]

The book I bought contained a sermon about Mary Magdalene which Adolphe Monod preached at Easter in 1850. The sermon started with a question: who did his hearers think should have been the first person to see the Lord Jesus after His resurrection? Whereas we might have thought of the Lord's mother Mary, or Peter, or John, the honoured person was in fact Mary Magdalene. This is made clear in Mark 16:9: "Now when He rose early on the first day of the week, He appeared first to Mary Magdalene, out of whom He had cast seven demons."

The sermon went on, explaining that Mary loved the Lord deeply because she was conscious of having had seven demons cast out of her. Adolphe challenged his listeners whether they truly realised how much the Lord had forgiven them. Did they understand what He had delivered them from? Did they love Him as Mary Magdalene had done?

I wish to consider this subject by focussing on what the Lord said to Mary Magdalene that day. Let me pose another question: what would you expect the Lord to speak about? He had been through tremendous suffering, and had voluntarily given up His life. What came out of the abundance of His heart (Luke 6:45)? We can find out in John chapter 20, verses 16-17:

> Jesus said to her, "Mary!" She turned and said to Him, "Rabboni!" (which is to say, Teacher). Jesus said to her, "Do not cling to Me, for I have not yet ascended to My Father; but go to My brethren and say to them, 'I am ascending to My Father and your Father, and to My God and your God.'"

This is a remarkable conversation. The Lord does not speak about Himself, or what He has gone through. Instead, He calls Mary by her name, thereby showing her who He was. This reminds me of John 10:3, "He calls his own sheep by name." And even then He does not speak to her of Himself. He speaks about His Father! His Father is now our Father. That is what He wanted her to tell His disciples. In short, that is what He was delighted about! This is perhaps one of the finest aspects of the fruit of His work.

It has often struck me how unselfish God is. While we do not see the actual word "Trinity" in the Bible, we do see God spoken of as the Father, the Son, and the Holy Spirit. Though we don't understand how God can be One and three Persons, the Bible shows a loving, "others-centredness" within the Trinity. The Father loves the Son and His plans are for His Son's glory. The Son loves the Father, and He loves His people. He said of Himself that He always did that which pleased the Father. The Holy Spirit unselfishly seeks to attract our hearts to Christ – He does not speak of Himself, but He brings the glories of Christ to us.

John 20:16-17 is one of these beautiful displays of that unselfish, loving character of God. The Lord Jesus is seen as the One who always seeks to bless. The Son of God is delighted to break the news that His Father is now our Father. We know that the Son really loved His Father (see John 14:31). We can also sense something of that love in John chapter 17, where He is praying to Him.

How delighted Jesus must have been to be going back to His Father's home, and yet here is the wonderful point: He is delighted that He can now righteously share that joy and that love with us! A couple of lines from a hymn express it beautifully:

> *That love that gives not as the world, but shares*
> *All it possesses with its loved co-heirs.*
>
> John Nelson Darby (1800–1882)

We should ask ourselves whether we fully appreciate this wonderful result of the Lord's work. Do we take it for granted? What does it mean that God is our Father? Our earthly fathers provide a good starting point for thinking this through. I am thankful that I do have a wonderful father, but sadly that is not the case for everyone – some fathers neglect their children. However, Jesus had good fathers in mind when He spoke about them in Matthew's gospel:

> Or what man is there among you who, if his son asks for bread, will give him a stone? Or if he asks for a fish, will he give him a serpent? If you then, being evil, know how to give good gifts to your children, how much more will your Father who is in heaven give good things to those who ask Him!
>
> **Matthew 7:9-11**

A good earthly father will not give his son something harmful in response to a request. What would we think of a father who gave his hungry son a stone to chew on? "Here, this will fill you up!" Or even worse, one who handed him a snake: "I haven't time to go fishing, so you can eat this poisonous snake!" Jesus points out that even though we are sinners, we generally know how to give good things to our children. Much more so will God give us good things!

Indeed, God is a God who gives. He gave us His Son. Paul sums it up in 2 Corinthians 9:15: "Thanks be to God for His indescribable gift!" When the Lord Jesus told Mary about her Father (John 20:17), He was telling her that a God who gives was now her Father!

Strangely, this giving character of God can be hard for us to understand. Surely we all love a gift, but we are often so used to earning and deserving things that we can find it hard to accept unconditional gifts from Him. We think that somehow we need to earn, repay or deserve what God gives us. But He gives because that is what He is like!

Consider the following verse in Romans 8: "He who did not spare His own Son, but delivered Him up for us all, …". How might we have expected that verse to continue? We might have thought something like this: "He who did not spare His own Son, but delivered Him up for us all, has given us a great gift, and we should be extremely grateful and not expect or ask for anything else." In fact, what this verse says is, "He who did not spare His own Son, but delivered Him up for us all, how shall He not with Him also freely give us all things?" (Romans 8:32). The One who gave us His Son is the One who will always give us good things! That is His character. This is our Father!

Of course, it is important to realise that this does not mean that God will give us everything we want. John Piper's insight in his book *Think* helped me with this point. Piper explains that Jesus says only what the father does *not* give – it does not say that the father *does* give bread or a fish, only that he does *not* give something harmful.[6] In the same way, God will not give us everything we ask for. What we want may be harmful for us, or we may be asking out of selfish or other bad motives. What we can be sure of is that God will never give us anything harmful. He only gives what He can use for our good and His glory, even if it may not seem like that when we receive it.

There are some verses in the Bible that might make us wonder whether God was not always our Father, and whether it really is a new relationship that has been brought to us as a consequence of Christ's work on the cross. However, if we consider how the Fatherhood of God was known to Israel in the Old Testament, we see that it was known in a national sense, without the individual relationship of each one to God as towards his Father. Consequently, God was not generally addressed as "My Father" in the Old Testament. There are but three Old Testament scriptures where God is referred to as "My Father". Two of these (Jeremiah 3:4 and 19) seem to relate to the nation of Israel as a whole. The other reference is in Psalm 89:26, but here this reference to David seems to point prophetically to the Lord Jesus Himself. Thus it was indeed a new relationship that the Lord Jesus brought in for us.

This new relationship appeared to confuse the disciples initially, since Philip asked "Lord, show us the Father" (John 14:8). Jesus replied, "Have I been with you so long, and yet you have not known Me, Philip? He who has seen Me has seen the Father; so how can you say, 'Show us the Father?'" (John 14:9). Philip found these things hard to understand, and so he wanted Jesus to show them the Father. Jesus' reply explained to Philip that Jesus Himself was the way to understand the Father. We have a good commentary on this subject in Paul's words in 2 Corinthians 4:6: "For it is the God who commanded light to shine out of darkness, who has shone in our hearts to give the light of the knowledge of the glory of God in the face of Jesus Christ." The Lord Jesus is the best, indeed the only way for us to understand God. We cannot see or know the Father any better than as we know Him through Jesus. What our Lord Jesus is like, the Father is like.

The Lord Jesus also shows us how we should relate to our Father. As we read through the Gospels, how do we see Jesus the Son of God relating to His Father? We see that He trusted in Him, He prayed to Him, and that His concern was to do the Father's will and to seek the Father's glory. He loved His Father, and He was confident of His Father's love for Him. Now the Lord Jesus is delighted to share that relationship with us: "I am ascending to My Father and your Father, and to My

God and your God." We, too, can trust in our Father; we can be concerned for His interests and His glory, and we can enjoy His love.

The Lord Jesus taught His disciples to pray to their Father, as we see in John 16:23-24: "And in that day you will ask Me nothing. Most assuredly, I say to you, whatever you ask the Father in My name He will give you. Until now you have asked nothing in My name. Ask, and you will receive, that your joy may be full." Further down in John 16:27 we read "for the Father Himself loves you, because you have loved Me, and have believed that I came forth from God." What we see is that God our Father loves us, and that He wants us to pray to Him. God the Father loves to give us blessings in response to our prayers, and we are encouraged to pray to Him. Now of course, this does not mean that we will get everything we want! We are to pray in Jesus' Name, which means that our prayers should be things that the Lord Jesus Himself would want for us, since we are asking with the authority of His Name.

Let's be encouraged to pray to God our Father. Let's also be watchful to see how He answers. A little while ago I read a book called *The Return of Prayers* by the Puritan writer Thomas Goodwin, who was writing in the 17th century. Even though it's an old book, its message is still current – we need to watch out for answers to prayer! This will help us to trust God more, and it will mean that God receives the thanks and praise that He should. If God does not answer in the way that we might have expected, it can also teach us to pray more in line with His purposes.

John chapter 17 is taken up with a wonderful prayer of Jesus Himself to His Father. There are many tremendous things in this chapter, but I will only focus here on verses 11 and 26. These verses read as follows: "Now I am no longer in the world, but these are in the world, and I come to You. Holy Father, keep through Your name those whom You have given Me, that they may be one as We are" (verse 11); "And I have declared to them Your name, and will declare it, that the love with which You loved Me may be in them, and I in them" (verse 26).

Here we have two great truths about our relationship with God our Father. God our Father will keep and guard us, and God our Father loves us. Let's rejoice in our Father's love and safe keeping, and let's not doubt it. A good father would want to protect his children, whom he loves. God our Father will keep our souls safe. He will make sure that we are brought safely to heaven. He gave His only Son so that we could become His children, and He will not abandon us. Some of God's children have gone through very difficult circumstances and times. They have not had easy lives, and some have even lost their lives because of their belief in God. But not one will have been lost for eternity – all will have been brought safely to heaven. John 10:27-29 gives us a wonderful summary: "My sheep hear My voice, and I know them, and they follow Me. And I give them eternal life, and they shall never perish; neither shall anyone snatch them out of My hand. My Father, who has given them to Me, is greater than all; and no one is able to snatch them out of My Father's hand."

Finally, we should consider that our Father has a home, and that is where we are headed for. Jesus said, "Let not your heart be troubled; you believe in God, believe also in Me. In My Father's house are many mansions; if it were not so, I would have told you. I go to prepare a place for you. And if I go and prepare a place for you, I will come again and receive you to Myself; that where I am, there you may be also" (John 14:1-3). The Lord Jesus was going to return to His home, His Father's house. But He was not going back there to be alone. We have a place prepared for us in our Father's home! What a wonderful prospect!

A Practical Application – our Worship

How should we respond to the revelation of God being our Father? One way is to joyfully take up our relationship with our heavenly Father, and trust in Him. We also have the privilege of worship. This is brought out in the conversation between the Lord Jesus and the Samaritan woman in John chapter 4:

> But the hour is coming, and now is, when the true worshippers will worship the Father in spirit and truth; for the Father is seeking such to worship Him. God is Spirit, and those who worship Him must worship in spirit and truth.
>
> **John 4:23-24**

These verses tell us about a quest: the Father is seeking true worshippers. We are perhaps more used to thinking of the Lord's quest to find those who were lost (see Luke 19:10), but the Lord Jesus surely must have rejoiced to seek and to save those who would become true worshippers of His Father. What a change – from sinners who were enemies of God, to forgiven saints who worship God in spirit and in truth! Once again I quote from a hymn:

> *Oh, counsel all divine to find*
> *True worshippers in those*
> *Who once, estranged by carnal mind,*
> *Were Thine and Jesus' foes!*
>
> R. Beacon (1819–1897)

QUESTIONS FOR REFLECTION

- What would you have expected the Lord Jesus to speak about on His first appearance after His resurrection?
- Have you considered the Father's quest for true worshippers as we saw in John chapter 4? How can we respond to this?
- What does it mean to you that God is now *your* Father?

Chapter 4
The Glorious Man

Look! I see the heavens opened and the
Son of Man standing at the right hand of God!
(Acts 7:56).

It was an amazing vision that Stephen had shortly before he was stoned to death. Luke the historian records it as follows:

> But he, being full of the Holy Spirit, gazed into heaven and saw the glory of God, and Jesus standing at the right hand of God, and said, "Look! I see the heavens opened and the Son of Man standing at the right hand of God!"
>
> Acts 7:55-56

In Stephen's vision, he saw "the Son of Man standing at the right hand of God". When you stop to think about it, we might not expect to see a man in heaven. Angels certainly, but man?

> What is man, that he could be pure? And he who is born of a woman, that he could be righteous? If God puts no trust in His saints, and the heavens are not pure in His sight, how

much less man, who is abominable and filthy, who drinks iniquity like water!

> Job 15:14-16

How could such a being be present in heaven? The mystery is solved when we consider who the Man is that Stephen saw. It is the Man Christ Jesus, who is at the right hand of God. This wonderful theme is fully brought out in Hebrews 2, one of my favourite chapters of the Bible. This chapter gives us the key to understanding Psalm 8, which it quotes, and thus the answer to Psalm 8:4, "What is man?"

Pause a moment and read Hebrews 2, and also Psalm 8. Psalm 8, read on its own, is a hopeful yet enigmatic psalm. In it we read that David was struck with wonder as to why God condescended to deal with man. He wrote of man being made a little lower than the angels, and yet crowned with glory and honour, with all things under his dominion. We instinctively think of the first man, Adam, who was created in the image of God, and who was set over all of God's creation. He was to rule over this earth as the representative of God. And yet, as we know only too well, this idyllic picture has been shattered. Adam succumbed to Satan's temptation and sin came into the world. Adam lost his crown, so to speak. All things are no longer under his dominion.

A friend of mine travelled to the Congo a year or so ago to encourage some of the Christians there. In one village, one man had lost an arm due to a crocodile attack. My friend related how he had been told of one crocodile that had been killed and in which had been found some wrist watches and five wedding rings. It had evidently attacked or killed at least five people! Truly, one cannot say that the beautiful picture of Psalm 8 holds true at this present moment.

Adolph Saphir, writing on the epistle to the Hebrews in the 19th century, explains how we can understand Psalm 8. I quote from him as follows:

> This psalm is evidently responsive to the original investiture of man with power when first created by God. God created him in His image, and appointed him to be the ruler upon earth. But does this explain the psalm? Let us look candidly, and say if this key is sufficient to open it. God's name is not now known over the whole earth; and this man, of whom the psalmist speaks as ruler, is it Adam? It cannot be Adam, because he does not speak of *man*, but the "son of man." ... But the apostle gives to us the key, that the psalmist speaks of the world to come, and of Jesus the Son of man ...
>
> **The Epistle to the Hebrews: an exposition, by Adolph Saphir (1831-1891)**[7]

By putting together Psalm 8 and its explanation in Hebrews 2, we see that the Holy Spirit is speaking to us about the world to come. In that world to come, the glorified Man Christ Jesus will be Head over all. Consequently, as we read Psalm 8 in the light of Hebrews 2, we start by thinking of Adam, the first man, and of what he was given and what he lost. We then move on seamlessly to consider Jesus, the "last Adam" (1 Corinthians 15:45). What Adam has lost, Jesus has more than recovered. What is more, *He associates us with Himself in the results of His work*. Truly He has re-written our history!

At the moment, "we do not yet see all things put under him" (Hebrews 2:8). The next verse continues with "But we see Jesus ...". What do we see when we see the Man Christ Jesus?

- We see Him as the Mediator between God and man (1 Timothy 2:5).
- We see the Last Adam restoring – and more than restoring – what Adam lost (Romans 5:15).
- We see that God has put all things under His feet (1 Corinthians 15:27).
- The Gospels show us a preview of His dominion: the triumphal entry into Jerusalem on a donkey, the miraculous catch of fish, the stilling of the storm, the withering of the fig tree, healing of diseases, overcoming death, casting out demons, and that He was not injured by wild animals (Mark 1:13).

We rejoice to see the glory of the Man Christ Jesus, but as we read further in Hebrews 2, we see that He has done all this for us![8] He tasted death for everyone (verse 9). He is the Captain of our salvation (verse 10). He is not ashamed to call us brethren (verse 11). He declares God's Name to us (verse 12), and surely this involves the revelation of the Father that we considered in the previous chapter. He shared in flesh and blood so that He might destroy him who had the power of death (verses 14-15). He did not take up the cause of the rebellious, fallen angels, but He takes up our cause (verse 16). He has become our merciful and faithful High Priest (verse 17). He is able to help us in our temptations (verse 18). He is not presented as the *unattainable example*. He is presented as *the Saviour* – the One who "restored that which He took not away."

Let us pause for a moment and remind ourselves of what we have seen so far about the results flowing from Christ's work on the cross. We saw in Zechariah's vision that the unsuitable can be made suitable for God's presence. We understand from the New Testament how this is possible, because righteousness is given to us, as indeed that great treatise on the gospel, the epistle to the Romans, teaches us right at the outset: "For in it the righteousness of God is revealed from faith to faith: as it is written, '*The just shall live by faith*'" (Romans 1:17).

We have seen how Christ's death and resurrection have brought us into a new relationship with God, so that He is now our Father, and how the Lord Jesus rejoiced to announce that wonderful result on the day of His resurrection. We have seen how Christ has re-written man's history, so that what Adam lost was more than restored in Him, and how we are associated with Him in His glory. Truly the results of His work are far reaching!

What shall we say to these things? To take up the words of the psalmist, "What shall I render to the Lord, for all His benefits towards me?" (Psalm 116:12). I find this best answered by a beautiful poem[9], part of which I quote here:

> *A homeless Stranger amongst us came*
> *To this land of death and mourning;*
> *He walked in a path of sorrow and shame,*
> *Through insult, and hate, and scorning.*
>
> *A Man of sorrows, of toil and tears,*
> *An outcast Man and a lonely;*
> *But He looked on me, and through endless years*
> *Him must I love – Him only.*
>
> Paul Gerhardt

QUESTIONS FOR REFLECTION

- How do you think about the Lord Jesus in heaven? Do you think of Him as a Spirit, or do you consider Him as a glorified Man – truly God and truly Man? What difference does it make?

- We started this chapter by considering Stephen's vision of Christ in glory. It is interesting to consider that one of Stephen's persecutors, Saul of Tarsus, later had a similar vision. Acts 8:1 states that Saul was consenting to Stephen's death. Yet not long afterwards, we read in Acts 9 how Saul was dramatically converted on the road to Damascus, as he too had a vision of the Lord Jesus in glory. How do you think that the vision of Christ in glory impacted Paul? Can you see this in his epistles?

Chapter 5
The Great High Priest

For Christ has not entered the holy places made with hands, which are copies of the true, but into heaven itself, now to appear in the presence of God for us (Hebrews 9:24).

Hebrews 9 tells us that Christ has come as High Priest of the good things to come (verse 11). Whereas the Old Testament priestly system showed that free access to God's presence was not yet open (verse 8), now we can draw near to God (Hebrews 10:19-23). This wonderful state of affairs is a consequence of Christ's finished work on the cross (Hebrews 10:12, 19-23) and is part of the fruit of His labour. Once again, we see with gratitude that the fruit of His labour involves our blessing, because having Jesus as our High Priest is exactly what we need (Hebrews 7:26).

What is a high priest, and what does he do? The recipients of the epistle to the Hebrews would have known of the first high priest, Aaron, as explained in the books of Exodus and Leviticus. An excellent summary of the *purpose* of the high priestly ministry is given in Hebrews 5 and 7:25-28. Some of these things are admittedly "hard to explain" (Hebrews 5:11), but let us not be afraid of studying them, because they are truly encouraging. I wish to consider three things in this chapter:

- The high priest is appointed *for men, in things pertaining to God* (Hebrews 5:1).
- Jesus was ordained as High Priest by God according to the order of Melchizedek (Hebrews 5:6).
- Jesus intercedes for us now in the presence of God (Hebrews 7:25).

Firstly, Hebrews 5:1 tells us that the high priest exists *for the benefit of men*, and *for the glory of God*. He is there to represent men to God, to stand in their place before God. He is also there to present our worship to God, and to deal with our sins. Exodus and Leviticus show that Aaron fulfilled this function. He acted as an intermediary between the people and God.

That he was there *for* the people is beautifully seen in his clothing. Exodus 28 presents us with the instructions that God gave to Moses for making Aaron's clothing. These clothes included precious stones with the names of the twelve tribes of Israel engraved upon them. An onyx stone was on each shoulder, with six names engraved on each stone. The breastplate had twelve precious stones, all different, in four rows of three, and each stone had the name of one of the twelve tribes engraved on it. In that way, Aaron symbolically carried the people on his shoulders and on his heart when he went into the presence of God.

To have a high priest who would do that must have been tremendously encouraging for the people. Firstly, it was God's idea – He had given these instructions to Moses. Therefore it was plain that God Himself wanted to bless His people, and had provided a way to do just that. Secondly, the fact that the names of the tribes of Israel were engraved on precious stones symbolised the value that God placed on His people – they were precious in His sight. The names were on the shoulder and the heart – and so God was looking for a high priest who would support His people, and care for them. The high priest would present their offerings and worship to God, and he would also officiate when sin needed to be confessed and a sacrifice for sin needed to be offered. We see this clearly in the first part of Hebrews 5:

> He can have compassion on those who are ignorant and going astray, since he himself is also subject to weakness. Because of this he is required as for the people, so also for himself, to offer sacrifices for sins. And no man takes this honour to himself, but he who is called by God, just as Aaron was.
>
> **Hebrews 5:2-4**

Now Aaron was a good man, but he was not perfect. The Old Testament clearly points out his sins, as well as his faithfulness. The verses quoted above show us that the high priest needed to offer sacrifices for his *own* sins as well as for the sins of the people. This meant that there was never that perfect freedom before God. The issue of sins still needed to be dealt with.

We can read in Exodus about how the tabernacle was to be set up – the place where God's presence would dwell among His people. The tabernacle had an outer court, and then a holy place, and finally the holy of holies, where God's presence and glory were. The holy of holies was not open to all. Only the high priest went in, and only once a year. Hebrews 9:8 tells us that this was to show that the way into God's presence was not yet made clear:

> Now when these things had been thus prepared, the priests always went into the first part of the tabernacle, performing the services. But into the second part the high priest went alone once a year, not without blood, which he offered for himself and for the people's sins committed in ignorance; the Holy Spirit indicating this, that the way into the Holiest of All was not yet made manifest while the first tabernacle was still standing.
>
> **Hebrews 9:6-8**

We, however, have Jesus as our great High Priest. Through Him we always have access to God's presence. Consider the great contrast between Hebrews 9:6-8 and the verses in Hebrews 10:11-23. As you read the latter, see how Jesus has taken away our sins for ever, and how we have free access – boldness even, as the Scripture says – to enter into God's presence. If we have never experienced the sense of being restricted from free access to the presence of God, we probably do not realise the extent of the blessing that Jesus has won for us through His work on the cross. He has consecrated that "new and living way" for us.

The second main point of this chapter is that Jesus was ordained as High Priest by God according to the order of Melchizedek (Hebrews 5:6). If we are familiar with the priestly system of the Old Testament, and with the history of Jesus of Nazareth as born into the house of David, we may wonder how He can be a priest. We see from Exodus that Aaron was chosen by God as the first high priest, and that this office was to pass on through his family. Aaron was from the tribe of Levi, and it was from this tribe, and from Aaron's family, that the high priest was to come. The Lord Jesus was born into the house of David the king, who was from the tribe of Judah. This is addressed in Hebrews chapters 7 and 8:

> For He of whom these things are spoken belongs to another tribe, from which no man has officiated at the altar. For it is evident that our Lord arose from Judah, of which tribe Moses spoke nothing concerning priesthood.
> **Hebrews 7:13-14**

> For if He were on earth, He would not be a priest, since there are priests who offer the gifts according to the law;
> **Hebrews 8:4**

Under the Old Testament law, it was not possible for just anyone to take up priestly functions. A striking instance of this is recorded in 2 Chronicles 26. There we read about King Uzziah, who had been greatly helped by God, but who presumed to take upon himself priestly functions, and went into the holy place to burn incense on the golden altar. The priests rebuked the king: "And they withstood King Uzziah, and said to him, 'It is not for you, Uzziah, to burn incense to the LORD, but for the priests, the sons of Aaron, who are consecrated to burn incense. Get out of the sanctuary, for you have trespassed! You shall have no honour from the LORD God'" (2 Chronicles 26:18). King Uzziah was furious, but he was struck with leprosy for his fault, as you can read in the rest of 2 Chronicles 26.

How then is our Lord Jesus Christ a high priest, since He is from the tribe of Judah, like King Uzziah was? The Bible tells us that *He is a Priest according to a different order – that of Melchizedek*. Who was Melchizedek, and what is the priesthood according to his order?

Melchizedek is introduced in Genesis 14, in just three verses:

> Then Melchizedek king of Salem brought out bread and wine; he was the priest of God Most High. And he blessed him and said: "Blessed be Abram of God Most High, Possessor of heaven and earth; and blessed be God Most High, who has delivered your enemies into your hand." And he gave him a tithe of all.
>
> **Genesis 14:18-20**

All we are told is his name, his kingdom, and the fact that he was priest of the Most High God. We see that he blessed Abraham, and that Abraham gave Melchizedek a tithe, that is, a tenth of his spoils. From these few details, however, the Holy Spirit has given us a wealth of interpretation in Hebrews 7.

Take some time to read Hebrews 7 carefully, and you will see how much we can understand about the Lord Jesus' priesthood from Melchizedek. Firstly, we see that unlike Uzziah, it was right for him to combine the offices of king and priest (Hebrews 7:1). His name and title mean "King of righteousness" and "King of peace" (Hebrews 7:2), which of course are truly fulfilled in the Lord Jesus. He has no genealogy, and is thus an illustration of the Son of God (Hebrews 7:3).

There are many genealogies in Genesis.[10] We know the family trees of most of the important persons written about – who their father was, who their descendants were, how long they lived. The genealogies of the priests were important, as we can see in Nehemiah 7:64 when some members of the priestly family could not function as priests after the captivity because they could not prove their family tree. The silence about Melchizedek, who suddenly appears in Genesis as a priest of God with no further explanation, is therefore significant.

Melchizedek's genealogy and the details of the length of his life aren't shared because Melchizedek is a picture of the Lord Jesus, the eternal Son of God, who is priest "according to the power of an endless life" (Hebrews 7:16). As Saphir says in his commentary on Hebrews[10], there is no point trying to work out who Melchizedek might have been, because it did not suit the Holy Spirit's purpose to tell us all the details of his life and background. His *apparent* lack of genealogy is there to illustrate the truth about the eternal Son of God, who has become High Priest according to Melchizedek for us.

Note that the announcement that Jesus is Priest according to Melchizedek is not simply a New Testament revelation. It is also a revelation that explains an Old Testament prophecy found in Psalm 110:

> The LORD has sworn
> And will not relent,
> "You are a priest for ever
> According to the order of Melchizedek."
>
> **Psalm 110:4**

This psalm was famously used by the Lord Jesus when He asked the Pharisees about the Christ in Matthew 22:41-46. He asked them how the Messiah could be at the same time the son of David and the Lord of David, and He silenced their further questions. This shows that it is really about Jesus Himself, who is both the root and the offspring of David (Revelation 22:16). Thus, in David's day there was already another priesthood, that of Melchizedek, which would be filled by the Messiah.

The third point of this chapter is that Jesus intercedes for us now in the presence of God (Hebrews 7:25). Hebrews 7 builds up an explanation of the Melchizedek priesthood of Jesus, giving us the wonderful truth of His intercession. We reach a climax in Hebrews 7:26: "Therefore He is also able to save to the uttermost those who come to God through Him, since He always lives to make intercession for them."

We need to understand the principle of intercession here. It does not relate to our sin after becoming Christians. That is dealt with in 1 John 1:18-19 and 1 John 2:1-2, where we see that Jesus is our *Advocate* when we sin. Here in Hebrews, the intercession is where Jesus, as the glorified Man who is our great High Priest, knows what help we need while we remain on earth, and sees to it that we receive the help and blessing required. This is summarized at the end of Hebrews 4:

> Seeing then that we have a great High Priest who has passed through the heavens, Jesus the Son of God, let us hold fast our confession. For we do not have a High Priest who cannot sympathize with our weaknesses, but was in all points tempted as we are, yet without sin. Let us therefore come boldly to the throne of grace, that we may obtain mercy and find grace to help in time of need.
>
> **Hebrews 4:14-16**

The Lord Jesus knows what it is like to be a man upon this earth – He "had to be made like His brethren, that He might be a merciful and faithful High Priest in things pertaining to God" (Hebrews 2:17). He has been along the pathway already, and He knows intimately the difficulties, discouragements and dangers that we can meet. Who better fitted to make intercession for us? This concept is beautifully expressed in a poem translated by Frances Bevan entitled *The Great High Priest*:[11]

> *Christ at God's right hand unwearied*
> *By our tale of shame and sin,*
> *Day by day, and hour by hour,*
> *Welcoming each wanderer in;*

THE GREAT HIGH PRIEST

On His heart amidst the glory,
Bearing all our grief and care;
Every burden, ere we feel it,
Weighed and measured in His prayer.

Fragrant thus with priestly incense
Each distress, each sorrow tells
Thoughts that fill the heart of Jesus
In the glory where He dwells.
All His love, His joy, His glory,
By His Spirit here made known,
Whilst that Spirit speaks the sorrows
Of His saints before the throne.

He, of old the Man of Sorrows,
Pleads before the Father's face.
Knowing all the needed solace,
Claiming all the needed grace.
We, so faithless and so weary,
Serving with impatient will—
He unwearied in our service,
Gladly ministering still.

T.P.

The poem expresses the wonder of the intercession of our Great High Priest according to Melchizedek. Just as Aaron bore the names of the Israelites on his heart when he wore the breastplate with the precious stones, so it is with Jesus: "*On His heart amidst the glory, Bearing all our grief and care.*" We often do not know what we really need, but He is described in the poem as "*Knowing all the needed solace, Claiming all the needed grace.*" What a strengthening thought that is! He knows what comfort, what help, what protection we need – because He has been through pain and suffering on this earth – "*He, of old the Man of Sorrows.*" He "claims the needed grace" for us.

Notice too the lovely way in which the ministry of the Holy Spirit is spoken of in this poem. He is the One who makes known to us Jesus' love, joy and glory, while He brings our sorrows to Jesus, so that Jesus can intercede for us before our loving Father. Truly, **God is for us** – God the Father, God the Son, and God the Holy Spirit! May we give our grateful thanks to our God and Father, through our Lord Jesus Christ, in the power of the Holy Spirit!

QUESTIONS FOR REFLECTION

- Do you think about the Lord Jesus interceding for you?
- How does it encourage you to think that He is asking God the Father for that which He knows you need?

Chapter 6
The Man of Joy

*Then I was beside Him as a master craftsman;
and I was daily His delight, rejoicing always
before Him, rejoicing in His inhabited world,
and my delight was with the sons of men
(Proverbs 8:30-31).*

In Genesis 29, we read the story of Jacob and his uncle Laban. Jacob wanted to marry Laban's younger daughter Rachel, and so he offered to work seven years for Laban for this prize. Verse 20 tells us that "Jacob served seven years for Rachel, and they seemed only a few days to him because of the love he had for her." Seven years is a long time, but it seemed short to Jacob because the prize at the end was so great in his eyes!

In a much greater sense, the Lord Jesus endured the cross for the joy that was set before Him (Hebrews 12:2). We know that He was a "man of sorrows" when here on earth (Isaiah 53:3), but now He has entered into His joy. Here indeed must be part of the fruit of His labour – that He is in His joy!

What do we know about this joy? I believe we have some hints and word pictures in the Old Testament.

However, let us first consider the New Testament teachings on the glory of the Lord Jesus after His death and resurrection.

- He was exalted to the right hand of God (Acts 2:33) and has been made both Lord and Christ (Acts 2:36).
- He was raised from the dead by the glory of the Father (Romans 6:4).
- When He ascended on high, He took captivity captive, and gave gifts to men (Ephesians 4:8).
- God has highly exalted Him, and given Him the Name above every name (Philippians 2:9).
- He was received up in glory (1 Timothy 3:16).
- He has the power of an endless life (Hebrews 7:16).
- He has the keys of hades and of death (Revelation 1:17-18).

These verses tell us something of the present glory of the Lord Jesus. It is good to think of Him in that way, after all that He suffered on our account. Yet, rather like the gospel accounts of the crucifixion, we are not told much about the feelings of our Lord. Just as we needed to turn to the Old Testament prophetic Scriptures (for example Psalm 22) to learn some of the depths of His sorrows, so we turn to the prophetic Scriptures to learn of His joy.

I believe that Psalm 21 presents some of that joy to us. If that is so, then it is interesting that it immediately precedes Psalm 22 – rather like the "joy set before Him" before the cross, as we see in Hebrews 12:2. Let us consider the first seven verses of Psalm 21:

> **To the Chief Musician. A Psalm of David.**
> The king shall have joy in Your strength, O LORD;

> And in Your salvation how greatly shall he rejoice!
> You have given him his heart's desire,
> And have not withheld the request of his lips.
> Selah.
> For You meet him with the blessings of goodness;
> You set a crown of pure gold upon his head.
> He asked life from You, and You gave it to him—
> Length of days for ever and ever.
> His glory is great in Your salvation;
> Honour and majesty You have placed upon him.
> For You have made him most blessed for ever;
> You have made him exceedingly glad with Your presence.
> For the king trusts in the LORD,
> And through the mercy of the Most High he shall not be moved.
>
> **Psalm 21:1-7**

In its primary application, this psalm of David is a companion, or answer, to Psalm 20. In Psalm 20, help is requested for the king, presumably before battle. In Psalm 21, the victory given by God is celebrated. But we can look beyond David to see David's Lord.

The True King, Jesus, rejoices in God's salvation. As we considered in Hebrews 5, Jesus "offered up prayers and supplications, with vehement cries and tears to Him who was able to save Him from death." In the language of Psalm 21, "He asked life from You", and the answer was given – "length of days for ever and ever." Thus we read of Jesus in Hebrews 7:16, being high priest "according to the power of an endless life." David did not literally have "length of days for ever and ever", as Peter reminded his hearers in Acts 2:29: "his tomb is with us to this day." We are therefore warranted to see a *prophetic* fulfilment of this Psalm in Christ, even if the *primary* application is to David.

What a joy, then, to see these wonderful words as having prophetic application to our Lord Jesus. I have put some suggested New Testament counterparts to them below:

The king shall have joy in Your strength, O LORD; And in Your salvation how greatly shall he rejoice! You have given him his heart's desire, And have not withheld the request of his lips. Selah. **Psalm 21:1-2**	Father, I desire that they also whom You gave Me may be with Me where I am, that they may behold My glory which You have given Me; for You loved Me before the foundation of the world. **John 17:24**
For You meet him with the blessings of goodness; You set a crown of pure gold upon his head. **Psalm 21:3**	I have glorified You on the earth. I have finished the work which You have given Me to do. And now, O Father, glorify Me together with Yourself, with the glory which I had with You before the world was. **John 17:4-5**
He asked life from You, and You gave it to him—length of days for ever and ever. **Psalm 21:4**	...Who has come, not according to the law of a fleshly commandment, but according to the power of an endless life. For He testifies: "*You are a priest for ever According to the order of Melchizedek.*" **Hebrews 7:16-17**
His glory is great in Your salvation; Honour and majesty You have placed upon him. **Psalm 21:5**	Therefore God also has highly exalted Him and given Him the name which is above every name, that at the name of Jesus every knee should bow, of those in heaven, and of those on earth, and of those under the earth, and that every tongue should confess that Jesus Christ is Lord, to the glory of God the Father. **Philippians 2:9-11**

For You have made him most blessed for ever; You have made him exceedingly glad with Your presence. **Psalm 21:6**	For David says concerning Him: *"I foresaw the LORD always before my face,* *For He is at my right hand, that I may not be shaken.* *Therefore my heart rejoiced, and my tongue was glad;* *Moreover my flesh also will rest in hope.* *For You will not leave my soul in Hades,* *Nor will You allow Your Holy One to see corruption.* *You have made known to me the ways of life;* *You will make me full of joy in Your presence."* **Acts 2:25-28**

What is striking about many of these New Testament counterparts is that they *involve the blessing of others: that is, the blessing of ourselves*. The Lord Jesus was received up into glory and is glorified by His Father, but He wants us to be with Him to behold His glory. He has become a high priest for ever according to Melchizedek, but He is our high priest, acting to represent us before God. He was made full of joy in God's presence, as Peter explains when he quotes the Psalms in Acts 2, with the result that the gift of the Holy Spirit was made possible: "Therefore being exalted to the right hand of God, and having received from the Father the promise of the Holy Spirit, He poured out this which you now see and hear" (Acts 2:33).

His joy involves our blessing. We should not be surprised. After all, He said of Himself in a parable, "And when he comes home, he calls together his friends and neighbours, saying to them, 'Rejoice with me, for I have found my sheep which was lost!' I say to you that likewise there will be more joy in heaven over one sinner who repents than over ninety-nine just persons who need no repentance" (Luke 15:6-7). Does He not rejoice over the prospect of us being perfected and in His presence? God's joy is spoken of in this manner in Jude verse 24: "Now to Him who is able to keep you from stumbling, and to present you faultless before the presence of His glory with exceeding joy."

What a marvellous picture all of this gives us of the character of the Lord Jesus: His principal joy intimately linked with our blessing! The apostle Paul instructs us in Romans 12:15 to "rejoice with those who rejoice, and weep with those who weep." Our supreme example in this is the Lord Jesus, who took our sorrows upon Himself and did something about it, and whose joy is in being able to bless us with the results of His work.

A Practical Application – Being Gracious to Others

Having considered the Lord Jesus entering into His joy, what about our response to Him? Are we interested in His affairs? Is our joy in His joy? Speaking for myself, I am sometimes uncomfortably reminded about my similarity to the prophet Jonah. Jonah is well-known as the prophet who was swallowed by a huge fish! But why did he end up in that predicament?

Jonah was a prophet who was told by God to go and preach in Nineveh, to warn the city that it would shortly be overthrown by God because of its wickedness. Nineveh was the capital of the Assyrians, the enemies of Israel. Jonah did not want to accept that commission, so he ran away, boarding a ship that was sailing to Tarshish. However, God caused a great sea storm to arise, and the sailors ended up throwing Jonah into the sea, at Jonah's own request. God prepared a great fish to swallow Jonah, whose life was preserved. The fish vomited him out onto a shore, and Jonah went to Nineveh to fulfil his commission. Amazingly, the city repented at Jonah's preaching, and so God's judgement was averted.

Why didn't Jonah want to go to Nineveh? We might assume it was because he was afraid to do so – after all, the Assyrians were known to be a cruel enemy. However, there is no indication in the book of Jonah that fear had anything to do with it. What is told to us, however, is Jonah's own reasoning for running away.

> ...God relented from the disaster that He had said He would bring upon them, and He did not do it. But it displeased Jonah exceedingly, and he became angry. So he prayed to the LORD, and said, "Ah, LORD, was not this what I said when I was still in my country? Therefore I fled previously to Tarshish; for I know that You are a gracious and merciful God, slow to anger and abundant in loving-kindness, One who relents from doing harm. Therefore now, O LORD, please take my life from me, for it is better for me to die than to live!"
>
> **Jonah 3:10 – 4:3**

Jonah had not wanted to preach to the Ninevites because he knew how gracious and merciful God was, and he was reluctant to give his enemies the opportunity to enjoy God's grace – he would have preferred to see his enemies destroyed!

Before we blame Jonah too much, we must remember that the Assyrians were well-known as a cruel enemy. They were a threat to Israel. And Jonah did not live in the New Testament dispensation of grace as we do now. But God wanted Jonah to know that *His* joy is in salvation, and that *He* desires the blessing of all men. Jonah sat out in the desert to see if Nineveh would be destroyed, and he got angry that it was not. While he was sitting in the desert, God made a plant to grow up and provide shade for Jonah, and Jonah was very grateful for that plant. However, God then made a worm that damaged the plant. The plant withered away, and Jonah had to suffer an easterly wind and the scorching sun (see Jonah 4:5-8). Jonah became pretty angry about the whole situation! God then spoke to him about it:

> Then God said to Jonah, "Is it right for you to be angry about the plant?" And he said, "It is right for me to be angry, even to death!" But the Lord said, "You have had pity on the plant for which you have not laboured, nor made it grow, which came up in a night and perished in a night. And should I not pity Nineveh, that great city, in which are more than one hundred and twenty thousand persons who cannot discern between their right hand and their left—and much livestock?"
>
> **Jonah 4:9-11**

God wanted Jonah to know how much He cared for people, and even the animals. Presumably the one hundred and twenty thousand who did not know their left from their right were small children. God cared for all, and wanted them to repent so that He could shower His grace upon them.

I generally find that this account makes for somewhat uncomfortable reading. We have seen together that the Lord Jesus is the Man of joy, and that His joy involves the blessing of others. That is what *He* delights in. Do I share in that aspect of His joy? Am I kindly disposed to fellow Christians, even if I find that they have hurt me?

They are, after all, that brother or sister for whom Christ has died, as Paul so beautifully writes in Romans 14:15. Do I care for the salvation of those who do not know Christ, even if they are not well disposed toward me? After all, He "is kind to the unthankful and evil" (Luke 6:35).

Still, it will not be in resolving to try harder, but rather in considering the Lord ever more, that I will become less like Jonah, and more like Jesus. "But we all, with unveiled face, beholding as in a mirror the glory of the Lord, are being transformed into the same image from glory to glory, just as by the Spirit of the Lord" (2 Corinthians 3:18). And let us not forget that Jonah himself was shown mercy and grace, in spite of his ungracious spirit. He is spoken of by the Lord Jesus Himself in Luke 11:32: "The men of Nineveh will rise up in the judgment with this generation and condemn it, for they repented at the preaching of Jonah; and indeed a greater than Jonah is here."

QUESTIONS FOR REFLECTION

- Do you think about the Lord Jesus entering into His joy?
- What does it mean to you that His joy is in providing for our blessing?
- How should we respond to His joy?

Conclusion
Putting it All Together

What then shall we say to these things? If God is for us, who can be against us? (Romans 8:31).

We have seen many beautiful aspects of the fruit of Christ's work on the cross. We have considered that His death and resurrection mean that our great need – our need for righteousness before God – can be met. Christ's work has fulfilled the Scriptures. He has taken our sorrows and our shame upon Himself, so that we can come into the promised blessings. His Father is now our Father, and He remains a glorious Man, who associates us with Himself in His glory. While we are still on earth, He graciously cares for each of His own as our Great High Priest. He was the Man of Sorrows on our behalf, and now He is the Man of Joy for our blessing. We truly agree with the words of Psalm 45:

> My heart is overflowing with a good theme;
> I recite my composition concerning the King;
> My tongue is the pen of a ready writer.
> You are fairer than the sons of men;
> Grace is poured upon Your lips;
> Therefore God has blessed You for ever.
>
> **Psalm 45:1-2**

PUTTING IT ALL TOGETHER

We have in no way exhausted the theme of the fruit of His labour. On the contrary, we have only begun. There is much more that could be said. Christ, through His work, has won His Bride, which is the Church (see Ephesians 5:25-32). God's ancient people Israel will come into rich and full blessing through Christ (Romans 11:26).

Today we live in the day of grace, during which God is graciously saving many as a result of Christ's death and resurrection. The tremendous gift of the Holy Spirit, the Comforter, has been given to us because of what Christ has done (John 16:7). To borrow the language of the apostle Paul, "What shall we say to these things?"

Certainly one important response is that of faith. All these word pictures of the work and character of the Lord Jesus that we have seen strongly encourage us to trust Him completely. We have every reason to trust our Saviour! Another response is worship, as we considered in Chapter 3. Furthermore, His love motivates us to serve Him, as we see in 2 Corinthians 5:14-15.

> God in heaven is holy, pure,
> Beautiful and radiant;
> I am of sinful heart—
> Sinful mind and sinful deeds,
> How could I be there?
>
> Jesus has come down to me,
> Holy, precious Son of Man,
> He has taken up my cause,
> He will bring me unto God,
> He will take me there.
>
> "Why have You shown love to me?
>   I who did not want to come,
>   I who loved my own desires,
>   I who loved myself?"

FRUIT FOR CHRIST'S LABOUR

"Pride had filled your sinful heart
So your wisdom was corrupt
And your eyes which could not see
Kept you in the dark.

In My Father's house above
There is light and there is joy,
There is fullness of His love;
And He wants you there.
I have this desire as well—
He and I are One.

So I suffered on the cross,
Took upon Myself all your sin.
Now I am a glorious Man
And you shall share in My estate—
Thus I bring you into joy—
All that I have won."

"Lord, such love is undeserved,
Wonderful beyond degree!
Overwhelming, absolute—
I cannot begin to tell
All its plenitude!"

God in heaven is holy, pure,
Beautiful and radiant;
I am there on Jesus' heart,
All accepted in His grace.
He has taken up my cause;
He has brought me there.

Yannick Ford

Appendix
Who is Jesus?

And when He had come into Jerusalem, all the city was moved, saying, "Who is this?" So the multitudes said, "This is Jesus, the prophet from Nazareth of Galilee" (Matthew 21:10-11).

This book has explored some of the marvellous results flowing out of Jesus Christ's death and resurrection. It may be that you have not really considered the life, death and resurrection of Jesus before. Who is Jesus, and why is He so important? Why do Christians make so much of His crucifixion? In this appendix I want to briefly outline a few reasons why a proper consideration of Jesus is so important.

The New Testament of the Bible contains the well-known gospels, namely Matthew, Mark, Luke and John. These books give four complementary accounts of the life of Jesus on this earth, which happened around two thousand years ago. There are some overlaps between the four gospels, but they are each written with a different emphasis in mind, so that by reading all four accounts we obtain a proper understanding of who Jesus is, and what He did.

It is thought that the gospels were written before the end of the first century[12], which means that they were produced not long after the crucifixion of Jesus. There is a fragment of a copy of John's gospel in The John Rylands Library in Manchester, which has been dated at approximately 125 AD. The fragment is from a "codex", or book that was found in Egypt. Since the apostle John is thought to have died around the end of the first century, the existence of this fragment shows that copies of John's gospel were already to be found in Egypt just a few years after his death. I have been to see this fragment, and it is fascinating to look at a scrap of ancient paper that must have been only a few copy numbers away from the original manuscript.

When I read the gospels, the picture of Jesus that emerges is that of a perfectly good man. It is worth studying carefully how He acted and responded in the varied situations described in the gospels. As I do this, I see someone who never acted in self-interest, but always to please God His Father, and always in the best interests of men and women. What He did and said was not always appreciated or popular – but it was always in the best interests of those who heard it.

It is often said that our strengths can also be our weaknesses, and vice versa. For example, consider someone who is confident and not overly concerned about what others may think about them. Such a person could be very good at passing on difficult messages when this is needed, but they may be lacking in tact on other occasions. On the other hand, a more sensitive person may be very good at listening to those who need reassurance and special attention, but they may not be honest enough with those who need to hear difficult truths! No doubt you could think of many such contrasts.

The description of Jesus in the gospels presents a perfectly even man. He was stern when He needed to be stern and compassionate and gracious when this was needed. He was angry when it was right to be angry, but calm and unprovoked when it was right to be so. I cannot do justice to this subject here, but I encourage you to read the gospels and see for yourselves the perfect responses of Jesus to every situation.

This leads me to pose a question: if you or I had wanted to write a fictitious story about a perfect man or a perfect woman, what would he or she have been like? Of course we would need to define what was meant by "perfect", but for the sake of argument, let's assume that we wanted to write about someone who always acted in the best interests of others, and who was not selfish or self-centred in any way. If we had never heard anything about Jesus, what kind of a person might we have invented?

It would be very hard to rise above our own imperfections, for a start. I can't speak for anyone else, but I know only too well how selfish and self-centred I often am! Not being consistently "others-centred" myself, I would find it difficult to write about an "others-centred" person. I could of course look for inspiration in other people, but as I mentioned earlier, it is often the case that our strengths can also be our weaknesses; our 'goodness' can also be our flaw. The writers of the gospels themselves did not hide their own weaknesses or those of their companions. It would be very hard to invent someone who *always* did the right thing in each circumstance, without leaning too far to the left or to the right.

Others have also recognised this difficulty. One such person was the Russian author Fyodor Dostoevsky, whose novels I used to enjoy reading (the English translations, of course!). One of them, *The Idiot*, has as its hero a good man called Prince Myshkin. Dostoevsky wrote to his niece about this novel:

> The basic idea is the representation of a truly perfect and noble man. And this is more difficult than anything else in the world, – particularly nowadays. All writers, not ours alone but foreigners also, who have sought to represent Absolute Beauty, were unequal to the task, for it is an infinitely difficult one. The beautiful is the ideal; but ideals, with us as in civilized Europe, have long been wavering. There is in the world only one figure of absolute beauty: Christ. That infinitely lovely figure is, as a matter of course, an infinite marvel (the whole Gospel of St. John is full of this thought …
> **Letters of Fyodor Michailovitch Dostoevsky to his family and friends**[13]

On reading the novel, I found that Prince Myshkin came across as a very likeable figure, but somewhat naïve. He did not really command respect, but rather sympathy. He is far from the perfect figure that Christ is. Indeed, Dostoevsky's own words are very telling, that the "infinitely lovely figure [of Christ] is, as a matter of course, an infinite marvel."

The depiction of Jesus in the gospels is indeed a marvel. In an initial reading of the gospels one might focus on the miracles that Jesus performed, but I have found as I read them again that it is His perfect response to every situation that is perhaps more miraculous. My opinion is that such a person could not have been invented. If that is so, then what we read must be the eyewitness accounts of the life of someone who really existed, and who really behaved as described. This is, for me, one of the strongest arguments convincing me of the truth of the Bible – Jesus as described in the Bible could not have been fiction, nor could accounts of His life have been embellished by later writers. I do not think that anyone could have risen above their own nature and written so convincingly about a perfect man.

What follows then is that I must take Jesus' claims seriously. If His appearance is an infinite marvel, as Dostoevsky states, then His words must be carefully considered. Jesus compared those who heard His words and put them into practice to those building a house on the rock, whereas those who heard His words and did not do them, like those building on the sand. He invites us to take Him at His word, as He says in Matthew 7:7 – "*Ask, and it will be given to you; seek, and you will find; knock, and it will be opened to you.*" While we will never fully understand God and all that He is, *He can be known*. Furthermore, He can be known *personally, through Jesus Christ*.

I was brought up in a Christian family. My parents taught me about Jesus from the Bible. I was attracted to Him as a person, but was not really willing to let Him influence my life too much. Thus, while I would have said that I believed in Him and His teachings, it would be honest to say that I kept Him at arm's length.

It was toward the end of my undergraduate studies that I became concerned whether I really believed these things. This is when I had to do the asking, seeking and knocking. I did not receive an answer straight away – it was only through reading the New Testament letter to the Romans several times that I became convinced that these things were true *and* that I had a true, living, personal interest in them: that is, they applied to me directly and personally. Since then I have consistently found that God has always been true to His word – not once has He let me down.

Do these things matter? As you answer this question for yourself, consider carefully the following passages from the Bible:

> And as it is appointed for men to die once, but after this the judgment, ...
> **Hebrews 9:27**

> Most assuredly, I say to you, he who hears My word and believes in Him who sent Me has everlasting life, and shall not come into judgment, but has passed from death into life.
> **John 5:24**

We read about a judgement after death in Hebrews, and we read about a way of avoiding that judgement in the Gospel of John. I would not like to be judged on my own merits! I may think that I have lived a good life if I compare myself with others, but not if I compare myself with Jesus.

I know that I am not perfect, and as such, I know that there is a distinct possibility that I will do, say or think something displeasing to God in the days and months ahead (perhaps rather in the hours and minutes ahead ...). I have fallen short of God's standard, and I will continue to fall short if left to my own devices.

This is no doubt why the prophet Isaiah felt so distressed when he saw a vision of God. There is nothing in the Bible to suggest that Isaiah was anything but a very good man, but when he saw a vision of God, He felt his own unworthiness:

> In the year that King Uzziah died, I saw the Lord sitting on a throne, high and lifted up, and the train of His robe filled the temple. ... ... So

> I said: "Woe is me, for I am undone! Because I am a man of unclean lips, And I dwell in the midst of a people of unclean lips; For my eyes have seen the King, The LORD of hosts."
>
> **Isaiah 6:1, 5**

How can this situation be resolved? How can I hope to stand in God's presence without being condemned? I may try to make amends for past sins, and seek to turn over a new leaf, but I will not be able to change my nature – I can never be sure that I will not fail again.

The answer is that God has fully provided for *all* our needs. We need to start again – we need to be *born again*, as the Bible terms it. The reason that the Lord Jesus came to this earth was **not** to provide us with an unattainable example – that would only have condemned us. He came instead to suffer the penalty that we should have incurred because of our sins. He came so that we could be made righteous and pleasing to God at His expense:

> For He [that is, God] made Him [that is, Jesus] who knew no sin to be sin for us, that we might become the righteousness of God in Him.
>
> **2 Corinthians 5:21**

That is why the Lord Jesus died on the cross – so that all that was and is wrong about me could be dealt with, and so that I could come into all that is good and blessed about the Lord Jesus. And so now the offer is open to all:

> Most assuredly, I say to you, he who hears My word and believes in Him who sent Me has everlasting life, and shall not come into judgment, but has passed from death into life.
>
> **John 5:24**

But it needs to be accepted if one is to benefit from it, and that has to be a personal decision. My hope is that you will make that decision.

Notes

1. See pp. 1976-1977 of *Unger's Commentary on the Old Testament* by Merrill F. Unger. AMG Publishers, Chattanooga, TN, USA, 2002.

2. *The Finding* by Heinrich Suso. In: *Hymns of Ter Steegen, Suso and Others* by Frances Bevan. James Nisbet & Co. Ltd, London, United Kingdom, 1894. Public domain material accessed on 20 November 2014 from https://archive.org/details/hymnsofterstee00beva.

3. See for example Matthew 26:55-56, 27:9-10, Mark 15:25-28, John 13:18, 15:25, 19:28, 19:36-37, Acts 3:18. There are a great many Scriptures that were fulfilled by the Lord's sufferings.

4. *We Would See Jesus* © Roy Hession Book Trust 1950, United Kingdom.

5. Quoted in: *Pages Choisies*, by Adolphe Monod, Editions des Groupes Missionaires, Vevey, Switzerland, 1959. The quote is cited as being from Adolphe Monod in Lyon, France, 1834, and is as follows: "Seigneur, conduis ma plume, et donne-moi des pensées et des paroles qui puissant glorifier ton Nom, nourrir ton people et convertir les pécheurs."

6. See pp. 51-52 in *Think* by John Piper. Inter-Varsity Press, Nottingham, United Kingdom, 2010.

7. *The Epistle to the Hebrews: An Exposition* by Adolphe Saphir. Gospel Publishing House, New York, USA, 1902. Public domain text accessed on 27 September 2014 from

https://archive.org/details/theepistletotheh00saphuoft.

8. This is not the whole story, of course. What our Lord Jesus did was for the glory of His Father, and in fulfilment of the Father's counsels regarding His Son. It was indeed also for us, but it is easy to become self-centred and think only of our blessing, even when considering these wonderful truths. However, I want to bring out the tremendous love and grace of God, brought to us by our Lord Jesus Christ, and to consider the wonder that we are associated with Him.

9. *Bands of Love* by P.G. (Paul Gerhardt) translated by Frances Bevan. In: *Hymns of Ter Steegen, Suso and Others* by Frances Bevan. James Nisbet & Co. Ltd, London, United Kingdom, 1894. Public domain material. Accessed on 22 November 2014 from https://archive.org/details/hymnsofterstee00beva.

10. See Chapter XV of *The Epistle to the Hebrews: An Exposition* by Adolphe Saphir. Gospel Publishing House, New York, USA, 1902. Public domain text accessed on 11 January 2015 from https://archive.org/details/theepistletotheh00saphuoft.

11. *The Great High Priest* by T.P. translated by Frances Bevan. In: *Hymns of Ter Steegen, Suso and Others* by Frances Bevan. James Nisbet & Co. Ltd, London, United Kingdom, 1894. Public domain material accessed on 20 November 2014 from https://archive.org/details/hymnsofterstee00beva.

NOTES

12. See Chapter 11 of *Nothing But the Truth* by B.H. Edwards. Evangelical Press, New York, USA, 2006.

13. Letter No 39 in *Letters of Fyodor Michailovitch Dostoevsky to his Family and Friends*, translated by Ethel Colburn Mayne. 2nd edition. The Macmillan Company, New York, USA, 1917. Public domain material accessed on 11 January 2015 from https://archive.org/details/lettersfyodormi00eliagoog.

FRUIT FOR CHRIST'S LABOUR

More Books from Scripture Truth Publications

Understanding the Old Testament series:

The Gospel in Job by Yannick Ford
  ISBN 978-0-901860-76-7 (paperback)
  ISBN 978-0-901860-77-4 (hardback)
  112 pages; March 2007

Understanding Christianity series:

Concerning Himself by John T Mawson
  ISBN 978-0-901860-92-7 (paperback)
  170 pages; March 2014

Thou Remainest by John Wilson Smith
  ISBN 978-0-901860-04-0 (paperback)
  100 pages; December 2013

www.ingramcontent.com/pod-product-compliance
Lightning Source LLC
Chambersburg PA
CBHW061340040426
12444CB00011B/3005